AGENCY SURVIVAL GUIDE

To: Craig

Katrina says great things about you. Enjoy this over a cold one (or two)

Cheers,

Max Traylor

Max Traylor's

AGENCY SURVIVAL GUIDE

How to
PRODUCTIZE CONSULTING SERVICES
and do other things better too.

VOL 30

Published by Max Traylor
max@maxtraylor.com
maxtraylor.com

Book Design by Kory Kirby

ISBN: 978-1-7348545-0-3

Printed in the United States of America

This book is dedicated to the brilliant
people that share their stories on

BEERS WITH MAX

DRINK | WATCH | LISTEN
MaxTraylor.com

CONTENTS

A PLEASURE TO WORK WITH YOU

Book Design
Kory Kirby

Book Illustrations
Ruben Ramos

Podcast to Book Concepts
Jonathan Rivera

Editor
Fen Head

GRATITUDE

Life
Robert "Bobby" Traylor, Robert "Bob" Traylor, Emily Traylor, Robert "Link" Traylor - my father, grandfather, wife and my son have given me the mindset and support to put LIFE first and inspire others to follow.

You pick me up EVERY time I fall down and that's a full time gig.
I love you.

My #2 at MaxTraylor.com
Katrina Busselle - you help me do what I do best, even better and you get everything else out of the way! I wish every entrepreneur had a #2 like you. Lucky.

Fillers of the Conversation Pipeline
Susan Tatum & Mindi Rosser - conversations fuel my business and this book. You've filled my calendar with incredible conversations, every week, for three years, without fail. Unbelievable.

Agency Partners
Joe Pettirossi, Kevin Jorgensen & Beverly Jorgensen - you all took a chance on me, gave me your trust and support. Together we created a digital, scalable, residual product where nobody thought to look. Forever grateful.

FEATURED INTERVIEWS

Jim Cathcart: Persistent focus and how to set yourself up to achieve
Page 12
https://bit.ly/JimCathcart30

Colleen Francis: The amazonification of sales and how its changing B2B buying behavior
Page 18
https://bit.ly/ColleenFrancis30

David C. Baker: Keys to agency success and selling your expertise
Page 26
https://bit.ly/DavidCBaker

Dr. Roxie Mooney, DBA: The effectiveness of focusing on a single business problem
Page 38
https://bit.ly/DrRoxie

Karl Sakas: How to escape the implementation black hole and become more profitable
Page 43
https://bit.ly/KarlSakas30

FOREWORD

When entrepreneurs lie awake at night thinking about their businesses, they will inevitably begin to dream about productizing their services. Rightly so, they are tired of crafting a different proposal every time, agonizing over how to price each engagement, and how to get in any sort of groove that allows them to solve recurring problems faster and better.

Then the next morning they slip back into order-taker mode and let prospects and clients self-diagnose, write their own prescriptions on a borrowed pad, and say adios. Sigh.

If you really know what you're doing, and if your positioning reliably feeds you prospects whose challenges you've seen before, it is not only a delight, but it is actually your duty to think about your business differently.

Max moves beyond the "wishing this was different" to some practical advice on how to make it happen.

This is a book that needed to be written.

— David C. Baker
Author of *The Business of Expertise: How Entrepreneurial Experts Convert Insight to Impact and Wealth*

———

HOW MUCH LONGER CAN YOU HOLD ON?

To people who make a living helping others grow their business: we consult, we strategize, we do things our clients can't do for themselves. It's a noble trade.

Yet most of us hit the plateau: in our business, in our personal income, in our lives.

It feels like this:

We're afraid to take on more clients because we can barely manage the clients we have. We try harder but we're running in place. Our motivation flame is flickering.

The truth is:

It's not our fault. The agency of record, time and materials business model, is dying and has been for a while. The rules have changed and if we're to thrive we need to change our mindset and focus on what is most valuable and difficult to replace: our knowledge.

This book is a collection of:

1. TRUTHS: Inarguable facts we need to come to terms with.
2. STRONG OPINIONS: Arguable, but likely winners.

Don't take my word for it...

After conducting hundreds of interviews over seven years with everyone from world influencers to struggling solo-preneurs who've given up on their vision:

These are their stories as much as my own.

HOW DO YOU MAKE THE MONEY?

We could all use more money. But what does money do for you? Will it buy you more peace? More free time? More happiness and fulfillment?

I remember being five years old and walking into my dad's home office. I asked:

"Dad, where do you make the money?"

I thought he was printing money. He didn't go to work like the rest of the dads. My friends rarely saw their fathers. Our family was different. We were spontaneous. We went to Disney World a lot.

Sadly my dad wasn't printing money. He told me that was illegal. What he did have was a business model that produced residual income.

"Digital, Scalable, Residual" he would say.

That was my lullaby.

A lot of people say that's a fairytale. It's not real life. We can't have our cake and eat it too. They tell us success is built on sacrifice. We have to settle. We have to work long hours for the man if we want a nice house, car, and to retire some day.

It doesn't have to be that way. I've seen it and lived it first hand. We can have our cake and eat it too.

If we put our personal life first, starting with what makes us happy, everything else will fall into place.

The reverse is also true. If we put work first everything else falls apart.

Why suffer so that one day we can retire from suffering? This has always seemed backwards to me.

These dynamics won't change until we change our priorities.

Here's an idea: prioritize your health and personal life.

Decide what you really want and what's most important to you. When you do, the money will figure itself out.

Money Tree

DIGITAL

When unsold products sit on a shelf, when employees sit around with no client work, it costs money. Every moment of rest eats away at profit margins.

Don't sell something that eats while you sleep. For my father's generation this meant don't put products on a shelf.

If you choose to do nothing,
If you choose to go skiing,
If you choose to take your son to Disney...

Make sure your business doesn't eat while you're away.

The traditional agency model says to buy people and put labor hours on a shelf. When those hours aren't sold, they collect dust, costing money. The business eats while we sleep.

If the model were a Sesame Street character it would be the Cashflow Monster.

The stuff of nightmares.

SCALABLE: A NEGATIVE "PAIN IN THE ASS" FACTOR

In professional services we know that the next dollar we make is more painful than the last.

Every client has different wants and needs and thus our work is different for every client. As we experience "success" we also experience the limitations of complexity. Our administrative overhead grows faster than revenue.

For a business to be enjoyed at scale it must have a negative pain in the ass factor: the more you make, the easier it is to enjoy life and provide value to the next client.

The next dollar must be easier than the last.

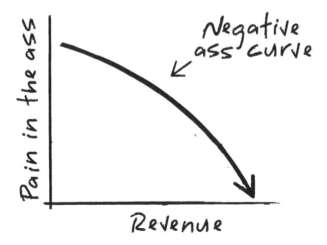

RESIDUAL

My personal favorite.

We have three relationships with money:

1. Project = do it once, get paid once
2. Recurring (or retainers) = keep doing it, keep getting paid
3. Residual = do it once, keep getting paid

As agencies we all celebrate the shift from project to recurring revenues because it reminds us of a steady paycheck: a safer, more civilized era.

Then we experience the limitations of complexity: the pain in the ass factor of putting unstructured and variable services into a long term contract.

The question we all need to answer for ourselves:

"How do I achieve a digital, scalable, and residual business model"?

$$\text{Project} = \frac{\text{\textcircled{L}}}{\$}$$

$$\text{Retainer} = \frac{\text{\textcircled{L}}}{\$\$}$$

$$\text{Residual} \neq \frac{\text{\textcircled{L}}}{\$\$\$}$$

THE MINDSET

Digital, Scalable, Residual is a mindset, a business mantra. The end result is not important, it's the mindset and the journey that leads us to better decisions.

If our goal is to "grow", or "double our business", we can get away with doing what we do today, just working twice as hard.

But when we put our personal life first, it forces us to do things differently.

The most powerful thing we can do for ourselves is define PERSONAL success. The business model should support our personal goals, not the other way around.

$$D + S + R = FREEDOM$$

MOTIVATION

My father wanted to be there for his son. He wanted to live, contribute to the world and be healthy.

When he put life first the only option was residual income: do something once and get paid forever. Detach time from income: negative "pain in the ass factor".

The truth is: you owe it to yourself.

RULE: The one and only, Choose Life First

So, what would you do with more freedom?

Jim Cathcart

Leading Expert on Sales and Motivation, Author of 20 books, Sales & Marketing Hall of Fame

"I've had breakthroughs over the years. They are always preceded by the decision to do something, and then eliminating the consideration of not doing it."

My take:

You, me, anybody can build a work life exactly as we want it.

Start with what you really want, the ideal, not with what you think is possible. Then make a list of all the challenges that stand in your way.

Most people will see these challenges as limitations and pursue the path of least resistance, inevitably landing them right back where they started: sacrificing life for work.

When you eliminate the consideration of not pursuing the ideal, all those challenges simply become a part of the plan, a part of your preparation, possibilities. This is where breakthroughs occur.

Listen to Jim Cathcart's full interview. We talk about limiting beliefs, focus, personal branding and his process for writing books.

https://bit.ly/JimCathcart30

PART I

—

THE RISE AND FALL OF AGENCY PRICE PREMIUMS

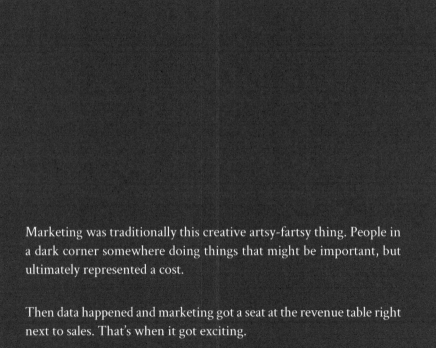

Marketing was traditionally this creative artsy-fartsy thing. People in a dark corner somewhere doing things that might be important, but ultimately represented a cost.

Then data happened and marketing got a seat at the revenue table right next to sales. That's when it got exciting.

DISCOVERING FIRE

Do you remember when you got excited about marketing?

It was my first business. We got some investors to give us money. Within two years we had spent all the money and didn't have enough customers to survive.

It was rough. It was painful. It was a big wake up call.

I had to confess that failure to investors.

New York, 2009, two years after graduating from Babson College in Boston, school for entrepreneurs. The investors told me: "The idea was great, but you don't know how to attract customers. You need to look into inbound marketing. You need to read up on how marketing can be used to drive revenue."

For non-marketers: "inbound marketing" just means marketing.

It doesn't matter how intelligent and talented we are, if we're not speaking to ideal customers on a regular basis, we won't survive.

Price premiums occur in marketing when we charge for results, not hours. It's a life and death trade just like sales. The closer to the money, the higher the premium we can charge. When marketing MAKES money clients pay us based on the value we deliver, not time and materials.

I don't know about you, but this is exactly what got me into marketing.

And it held true, until it didn't.

TRUTH: People don't buy your services, they buy the results.

So, what results do you sell?

Colleen Francis

Named in LinkedIn's Top Voices 2018, Hall of Fame
Keynote Speaker, Award-winning Sales Strategist,
Best Selling Author.

"People are more important to the buying process than ever before, [with social] their voices are magnified and there are more of them than ever before."

My take:

When the top names in sales strategy say that marketing is more important than sales in the buying process: well, that's a big change. And with change comes opportunity for new ideas, new methodologies, and new strategies for marketers to impact the bottom line.

I walked away from this conversation saying to myself: marketing agencies should act like sales consultancies.

After 5 years of interviews on both sides I can tell you for a fact that sales consultancies are more influential than marketing agencies.

Consultancies sell ideas, agencies take orders, yet both fight to achieve the same result.

Sell ideas, not hours.

Listen to Colleen Francis' full interview. We talk about the changes in B2B buying behavior and how to deliver ideas at scale to grow the business of consulting.

https://bit.ly/ColleenFrancis30

THE REPLACEMENTS

When I first started my agency, I was closing deals and pricing based on value relative to quantifiable results. I could do this because I wasn't being undercut by thousands of lookalike firms.

My team and I had special training. We had special skills.

I got scared in August 2012. The day I realized I was replaceable. It was Hubspot Partner Day.

If you've ever been a "channel partner" or "value added reseller" for a marketing or sales technology company, you've seen it too. Partner day was a sea of lookalike agencies, a galaxy of indistinguishable stardust, an army of marketers trained to sell and service clients just like me.

It took me four years and way too much money to understand the concept of REPLACEABILITY.

A college degree used to stand out. It meant something. Today you spend four years becoming a specialized, sought after resource, then sit shoulder to shoulder with thousands of people on graduation day ready to do the same job for less and probably work harder, at least in my case.

The system survives on belonging, comfort, and confidence: confidence in the process - a proven system. It has to work. It works for everybody!

In reality we accept lower pay than the next graduate and we'll overwork ourselves to keep whatever job we get.

This is exactly what "partner day" feels like... if you stay sober.

Serious money is going into training our replacements.

In the past decade alone marketing has seen more than one "bubble": a sudden inflation of prices due to increased demand without the supply of products and services to satisfy the need. Remember kids: every bubble pops.

The first bubble was marketing software: new tech to drive business growth.

The software bubble caused a brief labor bubble.

Software companies need an army of button pushers to sell and service their products. Partners (Value Added Resellers) are cheaper than employees, so they dumped millions into training programs.

Value Added Reseller programs are meant to make us REPLACEABLE. Without interchangeable parts and standardized services the SaaS model (Software as a Service) falls apart.

Every lookalike agency, "certified" freelancer and digital marketing grad increases supply and decreases the price we can charge.

The bubble deflates and the premium on marketing services disappears.

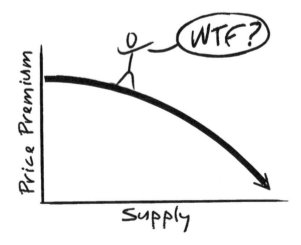

COMPETITIVE DISADVANTAGE

My first hire as an agency owner was a former editor of a local newspaper. Content was king, and I wanted a secret weapon, an in-house writer.

When the writer couldn't handle any more work, which took about a year, we looked for another. It was freakishly easy this time. oDesk, eLance, Upwork, all of these online forums with thousands of freelancers that can write, that can design, that understand marketing automation, had popped up seemingly overnight. The freelance gig network had exploded across every corner of marketing services.

Upwork alone has 12 million freelancers.

The Bureau of Labor Statistics (BLS) called the freelance gig network the "industrial revolution of our time".

From my perspective I saw my biggest investment to date go from a competitive advantage to a competitive disadvantage in the same year.

The truth is when clients think they can pay less for the same work, they will.

THE OWNER'S COUSIN JUST GRADUATED

I was on top of the world. Inbound marketing really works! One client stood out, they made password protection software. We got them incredible results and fast. When people asked for a reference, they were the obvious choice. Lets say they made 10x their investment with us in the first six months.

I'll never forget the phone call...
"Max you've done great work for us but we need to bring it in-house."

You're all too familiar with the confusion and brain rage that followed:

"How could they bring it in-house? How could my client be so naive, so stupid to think that the owner's cousin who just graduated can do what I can do. They can barely find their way out of the bathroom. I have years of experience, I'm special!"

That's the way we all feel the first time. The second time we question ourselves.

Clients are bringing the work in-house: design, SEO, copywriting, social media. It's like standing behind someone on a diving board knowing they can't swim but they sure as hell know how to jump and that makes them dangerous.

We can't stop them. Clients WILL bring what you do in-house. Why? Because they THINK they can. The specialized labor, the limited resource, the time and materials we could charge a premium for is now a commodity.

A race to the bottom.

DECISION MAKERS AND ORDER TAKERS

I think every professional marketer would agree that we are strategic partners in our clients' businesses: decision makers.

But what do clients think?

Do they see us as decision makers or order takers? There's no grey area.

We start out decision makers. During the sales process our prospect will ask for our opinions and ideas. We analyze their pains. We come up with tailored solutions. We create a plan. We coach their team to see what we see and think how we think. If we get the business, it means we were a decision maker–in that moment.

My official title at the agency was 'Lead Strategist'. During the sales process prospective clients would introduce me to other members of the buying committee:

"This is Max, he will be helping us with our marketing strategy."

Yet as time went on each client would refer to me differently. I've been called a blogger, website developer, designer, social media specialist, email marketing guru... all of it.

Whatever I was doing at the time was how they introduced me.

IT'S A SLIPPERY SLOPE

When it came time to be strategic again, to be a decision maker, they would fight me. I had lost control.

They didn't see me as a strategist anymore. I was demoted to an order taker.

This is built into business culture: the hierarchy. There are three levels:

The top level makes decisions
The bottom level takes orders
The middle makes sure the bottom follows orders

Our clients have been culturally trained to put us into one of these buckets and we can only be in one at a time. Remember their goal in life is to move up which means they need people to fall in line below them.

Thus we are relegated and seen as the lowest value task that we take on. It's easy to go down, extremely hard to go up.

The truth is: if we want to charge a price premium we have to be in control, we have to be decision makers. We can't say YES to everything.

Strategy, consulting, and planning is where decision makers live. This is where price premiums survive in even the most saturated of markets.

Value is the key to price premiums.

Replicability is the enemy of price premiums.

We need to sell what is most valuable and difficult to replace.

$$\frac{Value}{Replaceability} = Price\ Premium$$

STRONG OPINION: Sell ONLY what is most valuable and difficult to replace.

So, what do you have that is most valuable and difficult to replace?

David C Baker

Author of The Business of Expertise and called "the expert's expert" — NY Times. Advises entrepreneurial experts.

"The implementation side of the business is just being picked up and moved over to the client side."

My take:

The Business of Expertise is the best book for entrepreneurs and agency owners who want to sell what is most valuable and difficult to replace.

We have to shift our mindset because "doing" the work is replaceable. If the implementation is being brought in house, our expertise is all we have left.

The shift: expertise IS the product and it is the most unique and powerful product we have to offer.

This will always be one of my favorite and most personally valuable interviews.

Nothing short of life changing...

"Develop all your insightful observations into a system. Price it as a diagnostic package, and now you have a real process that is likely different from all the "me too" processes that have spread like weeds on websites." — 226 Business of Expertise

Listen to David C Baker's full interview. We talk about price premiums in implementation vs strategy and how to position yourself for sustainable success in a constantly changing agency landscape.

https://bit.ly/DavidCBaker

PART II

—

SELLING STRATEGY

In January 2013 my partner manager at Hubspot asked if I could save 20 accounts that were cancelling their subscriptions.

I was forced to sell something different. These people had all the ingredients: the software, the content, even people trained to make it work.

They had the ingredients but no recipe. No cook book for turning the ingredients into results. They needed a plan.

They were pissed, which intimidated me. But they only had two choices, which gave me confidence:

A: Cut their losses: years of work, hundreds of thousands invested.

B: Bring in a chef.

A PLAN

I sold a plan. Then another, and another. I wish I had that little red Staples "easy button" because IT WAS EASY. I sold it for $2,500 the first time.

Their feedback: "Hey, this was worth it. This was worth it because we've spent so much on content and technology that wasn't working for us. We needed a plan to make it work."

I sold 10 plans in a month. To service 10 clients by myself the process for producing the plan had to be efficient and repeatable. A single 90 minute workshop to gather information and a 30 page mad-lib style strategy template with spaces where words could go, was all I could handle.

Workshop: 1.5 hours
Fill out the mad-lib: 1 hour
Present the plan: 1.5 hours

The plan included goals, team roles, activity timelines and a monthly budget for implementation services.

So essentially 4 hours of work to sell implementation services: something I was all too accustomed to do for free as a necessary cost of sale.

This time I got $2,500, up front, to do the same thing!

$625 per hour. Every other service we were billing out at $200 per hour.

A clue, Sherlock!

I learned two things:

1. Strategy, the how to, the planning, was more valuable than implementation because without it they would have nothing to show for their time and money.
2. Products are more profitable than services: consistent inputs and outputs. Like an iphone that's tailored to each user but with the same hardware and operating system.

PRICED LIKE AN INSURANCE POLICY

Nobody needs dental insurance until they smash their teeth in.

Strategy and planning is essentially an insurance policy. It ensures the clients' investment in marketing is going to achieve the desired result.

As such, the amount a client is willing to pay for strategy is directly related to the clients' implementation budget: full-time employees, contractors, content, technology, ad spend and so on.

My recommendation is to charge between 10% and 20% of whatever they are spending to get disappointing results.

Of course, for people that don't currently spend money on marketing, strategy holds very little value. To these people the planning stage is an obstacle.

We can see them coming a mile away. They want to get started. They want people that can do the work fast and cheap. They want the basic version of the software.

Go find clients with their teeth smashed in, they're easy to find. Just look for lots of content and expensive websites.

Follow the money.

$$\frac{Current\ Spend}{10} = Good\ Guess$$

WELCOME TO THE REVOLUTION

Never again.

I realized that when the Bureau of Labor Statistics was talking about the "industrial revolution of our time" there would be winners and losers.

The losers would take their spot on the assembly line. They would say: "Great, I would love to create that content. I would love to build that website. I would love to push buttons in your software all day. That would be perfect. Get paid a little, work a lot, but hey, it's a job."

The winners in the industrial revolution played a different game. They created and sold systems. A process to get the most return from com-moditized labor and interchangeable parts. All things being equal: the system is the competitive advantage.

Ford did it then. Uber, Amazon, Airbnb and YOU can do it now.

WHO WILL PAY YOU THE MOST?

My first strategy product was called the Content Marketer's Blueprint™: a repeatable system and three-month action plan for attracting ideal customers and nurturing them to a point of sale.

The "CMB", as we called it, was specific to content marketing and the software product it supported, but not specific to any particular industry.

It easily sold for $2,500.

Three months later we sold the same exact strategy, same workshop, same deliverable, same system for $30,000.

The only thing that changed was how we positioned it. We changed some words to align the product with our prospect's industry: higher education, a college.

I literally replaced the word "lead" with "prospective student" in the templates and multiplied the price by ten.

Explain that:

A college's investment in marketing is relatively high. They have full time team members which means they spend a LOT of money for disappointing results.

But the MEGA-PREMIUM came from a reduction in replaceability.

At the time, April 2013, to find someone who was selling content marketing strategy without jamming software and content down your throat was difficult. But finding a specialist in content marketing for higher education: well, they didn't exist.

There was nothing to compare me to. I was in control.

FOCUS: THE MEGA-PREMIUM

Focus amplifies value because it counteracts replaceability. End of story. Want to charge more? Solve a specific problem for a specific kind of company.

You can stop reading now... go do that! The rest will fall into place.

The reason we don't take our own advice without significant third party therapy is fear and hunger. Fear of missing out and our hunger for the next paycheck.

I resisted focus. I was "deal hungry" but the decision was made for me. I inherited higher education as a focus from my business partners who'd worked in the space for years.

I got lucky.

That said, I quickly decided I never wanted to work in higher education, ever again. It was the exact opposite of what I wanted: "decision by committee" made me sick. I don't have the patience for it. I don't want to explain my recommendations to eleven people. I just want them to follow my F-ing directions! Just give it a try!

Higher education was the complete wrong space for me.

Yet the moment I chose to take a risk and focus on higher education I commanded a 10x price premium for the exact same process. Focused messaging, not the amount of work, not a more complex process, just different packaging made it more valuable to the client.

Lexus is basically Toyota. Packaging.

I digress: choosing the wrong thing cured me of not focusing.

I chose the wrong thing another two or three times and I loved every minute of it. Each failure funded a pivot. Each pivot got me closer to the answer.

Give yourself a free pass to focus on the wrong thing.

Enjoy the ride.

TRUTH: Focusing on the wrong thing is better than not focusing at all.

So, who will pay YOU the most?

Dr. Roxie Mooney, DBA

Creator of the COIQ™ Early Adoption Framework & international best-selling author of *How Health Innovators Maximize Market Success: Strategies to Launch and Commercialize Healthcare Innovations*

"I was focused on healthcare innovators and specialty pharmacy, but even those submarkets were getting saturated and commoditized. To protect our differentiation, we had to narrow our focus to a specific business problem for one of those audiences."

My take:

Dr. Roxie is my favorite example of how focus can lead to price premiums, authority, and influence.

The first thing she was asked to do when getting her doctorate in business was to identify a specific problem with an unmet need. In academia, and in business practice, you're only considered an expert when you narrow your focus on a specific industry or sub-industry AND a practice area or business problem.

Everything else has been done before, and you'll just be a me-too company.

This is an incredible mindset for business leaders chasing price premiums and a defensible competitive advantage.

Dr. Roxie offers one strategic process called the COIQ™ Early Adoption Framework in multiple formats that vary in price and scalability. Her healthcare innovation strategy products and services include group coaching, workshops, online courses, and of course, one-on-one consulting engagements with a BIG price tag.

She's inspired me in a number of ways but most of all I feel lucky to have a front seat view to watch her business transform and to be a part of the emotional challenges and breakthroughs along the way.

Watch Dr. Roxie's full interview. We talk about being hyper focused and the fear that comes with it.

https://bit.ly/DrRoxie

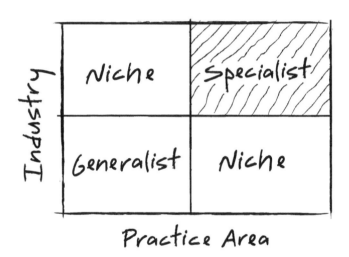

STRATEGY VS. IMPLEMENTATION: FIGHT!

Three years went by. Every client got a productized strategy and in most cases we implemented it for them.

By January 2016 my new years resolution was:

"I will give all implementation contracts to our competitors for a revenue share."

When my business partners didn't see what I saw I turned in my keys and told them I would be more valuable to them on my own. Looking back I can see the position I put my partners in: we had employees and had to make payroll. It was me or the employees.

Ever walk away from something you've spent four years creating? I told them over breakfast. Two eggs OVER MEDIUM with extra crispy home fries. I cried.

I'm on my own now: "Hi, I'm Max. I make marketing plans."

At MaxTraylor.com I sold and delivered strategy. My official title at my clients' organization was strategist. Did I touch implementation? Absolutely not.

Why?

Because with strategy in hand I could give the implementation to any agency I wanted and they would pay me 10-20% of revenue in perpetuity. That means forever.

This "residual" income was 2-4x the profit margin of doing, or managing the implementation myself.

THE NUMBERS DON'T LIE

Sell the plan you currently give away for free during the sales process or early in your client engagement. Sell the thing you know is most valuable. The thing that sets you apart from the e-lancers. Sell it by itself.

Don't bundle! That's cheating and defeats the purpose. Remember you are seen as the lowest value task you perform. Bundle strategy and implementation and you'll be seen as an implementer.

Sell strategy and enjoy increased control over your implementation engagement. This means operational efficiency, which is good enough to add a few percentage points to the bottom line. I was very excited by this. I celebrated. New Callaway XR golf clubs I believe.

But, if you take my advice and sell strategy by itself, it is very important that you compare strategy with implementation as I did.

How much did you make?
How much effort did it take?
How did it make you feel?
How do your clients introduce you?

The only legitimate downside comparing the two is that implementation represents ongoing revenue, safety, a retainer. Strategy is just a project.

If it were possible to sell strategy, planning, and consulting as a retainer would you give up implementation?

STRONG OPINION: Burn your implementation business to the ground... figuratively speaking.

List the reasons why YOU need to do the implementation.

Karl Sakas
Agency consultant and executive coach

"Every agency service fits into one of three categories: think, teach and do.

Do - is the lowest margin activity because it is easily commoditized, but it is easy to sell.

Think - is harder to sell because you are selling intangibles. Highest margin but if you are an order taker they won't trust you to do strategy.

Teach - is an interesting opportunity because more and more clients are bringing the "doing" in house. It can be highly profitable because the training you do for one client can be applied to the next."

My take:

Karl has a brilliant financial mind. He knows the numbers that kill agencies and sap the energy from their brilliant strategists.

I don't think he would go as far as to say "burn implementation to the ground", but he would encourage you to understand that when you "do" the work, there is an opportunity cost.

Listen to Karl Sakas' full interview. He explains some key financial metrics to health check your agency and how to escape the implementation black hole.

https://bit.ly/KarlSakas30

PART III

BEING INDISPENSABLE

People say: "But Max, strategy without implementation is useless".

Me: "Brilliant!"

Strategists should focus on strategy. Implementers should focus on implementation. In order for these separate roles to function as a team, two things need to be true:

The strategy is actionable: it contains step-by-step directions and all the resources necessary to implement the plan.

Someone out there in the world has the ability to follow your directions.

Do both roles need to be under the same roof?

ding ding ding

I'll take "limiting beliefs" for $1,000!

REPLACEABLE VS. INDISPENSABLE

Rhetorical Question: Does the coach of the team go onto the field?
No, the coach stays on the sideline and thinks about how to win.

Rhetorical Question: Does the pirate ship captain go below deck?
No, he reads the stars and steers the ship.

Players and pirates are replaceable.
Coaches and captains are indispensable.

These roles cannot mix. If we display the behavior of a strategist and an implementer, our clients will always see you as an implementer. Always the lesser of the two.

Becoming indispensable requires a separation of strategy and implementation.

If we offer both, they need to be separate: separate cost, separate people, separate conversations. Else we leave it to our clients to decide how they introduce us to the boss.

DO NOT BUNDLE!

I bundled...

In my "hybrid" days I started every client with strategy and moved them to implementation. At some point during implementation I would get a breakup email from even my top performing clients. Sometimes it would take six months, others longer.

Contract length rarely mattered. False sense of security.

They said: "we have made a decision to go in a different direction."

When I bundled strategy and implementation I was giving my clients a choice: was Max going to be an order taker or a decision maker? Replaceable or indispensable?

When doing strategy we have a seat at the table. We are decision makers. When managing implementation, we lose our seat at the table. We become order takers.

How quickly they forget.

$$\text{Strategy} + \text{Implementation} = \text{Implementation}$$

The only way to keep your seat at the decision maker table is to charge separately for your ONGOING role as a strategist.

Every time our clients cut a check they must be reminded that they are paying us to help them make decisions.

Let me be clear: you need a separate line item for strategy, planning, consulting, or decision support, in your proposals and service level agreements which extends for the entirety of your engagement.

Why would someone continue to pay us for strategy?

Because a plan is only as valuable as the information we have available at the time. It is a living breathing thing. As we gain more information, conduct more experiments, interpret results, we get smarter. Plans need to be adjusted. New opportunities and challenges need to be considered.

A coach doesn't come up with a plan at the beginning of the season.

The coach comes up with a plan for every game.

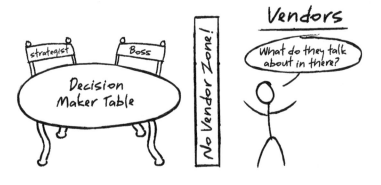

VENDOR EVALUATION

If we get paid for both strategy and implementation, our clients will fire us for both, not just one.

This happened to me all the time in my "hybrid days".

But then I got a very different email from a strategy ONLY client:

"Max, I want to fire our agency. I'd like to talk to you first before we do anything".

Bias! Bias is the lesson.

If you offer strategy and implementation your clients won't include you in decisions about hiring and firing vendors. You ARE a vendor!

What did I change?

For this client I added "Vendor Evaluation" as part of my strategic service. It was a power move to ensure there would be no confusion about my status as a strategist vs a vendor.

And guess what: they always introduced me as a strategist!

The truth is: where to spend money and with whom is one of the most important decisions our clients make. Agencies, vendors and implementers are not a part of this decision. We need to be a part of it.

You figure it out.

TRUTH: Strategy is NOT a one time thing.

So, what decisions do you help
your clients make over time?

Steve Lishansky

Strategic Mentor and Advisor to CIOs and CEOs, author of The Ultimate Sales Revolution and creator of the Indispensable Partner™ Framework.

"Your job is to be a facilitator of what is most important... the problem is that most times the other person doesn't know what is most important."

As a client and a mentor, Steve helped me clarify the ongoing role of a strategist.

If we want to create a long term strategic relationship with our clients and continue to command a price premium, we must establish and maintain our status as an indispensable partner.

In his book *Ultimate Sales Revolution* Steve says this about selling yourself as an indispensable partner:

"There are two important perception shifts that are critical to facilitate with your clients.

Your client perceives that you understand what is most important to them.

Your client perceives that you can help them take care of what is most important."

NOTE: "Take care of what is most important." Not "do it yourself".

Listen to Steve Lishanky's full interview. We talk about the Indispensable Partner™ process and getting paid for your value by finding the right clients that are willing to invest in the right results.

https://bit.ly/SteveLishansky30

CONTROL

Most people I meet aren't driven by money, they are driven by contribution. They want to make a difference in their clients' lives. They want to help their clients' businesses grow. They're not selfish people. In a lot of ways, they're selfless.

We like to provide as much value as possible during the sales process. We do this to impress, we do it to build trust and we do it to win the deal. It feels good.

I would help my clients evaluate their situation. I would give them detailed action plans. I would tell them exactly what they should do, when they should do it and in what order. I spent hours doing this. It took months to sell these engagements.

At the end of this process I found myself in a negotiation. There was a picking apart of my recommendations. Either price or scope.

"Max, I think we should do this. I don't really know about this part over here. I think we have somebody who can do this piece. It's not the right time for that thing..."

Silent mumbles: "are you kidding me? Like, wait a minute, you're interested in working with me because of my expertise, right? For months I've been working on putting together an action plan tailored to your situation. Now we're having a conversation about why my recommendations aren't what you need."

BAD DOG!

I have a golden retriever, his name is Dr. Leo Marvin. Yes, as in Richard Dreyfuss's character in What About Bob starring Bill Murray. He's a good boy.

When I was training Dr. Marvin the breeder said: "don't give him treats for nothing. Make him do a trick. Make him sit, make him bark, make him rollover. Make him do something! If you don't, he'll expect treats for nothing and he'll never listen."

I'd treated my clients like pets. I loved them! I gave them treats for nothing and it felt good. Then three months later they expected the strategy for free. AND they wouldn't listen!

The truth is: if someone pays us to help them make decisions they listen or they fire us. People that get our advice for free have no obligation to take that advice.

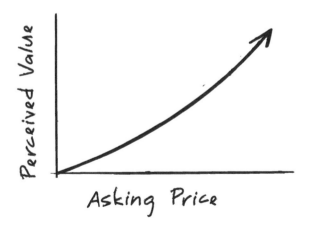

OUR OBLIGATION TO CLIENTS

It's most important that both parties, they the buyer and we the seller, understand that our knowledge and expertise is our most valuable contribution. We make our clients pay for it because it is our obligation to ensure our recommendations are taken seriously.

TRUTH: Free = not valuable.

So, list the things you do for free.

Kristen Ortwerth
Marketing Consultant & Advisor

"The most rewarding thing in my career is being able to say to clients: these are the boundaries, this is the path, what's at the end of this path nobody knows, but we are going to go explore that together but we are not going to spend a lot of time going down rabbit holes along the way."

Kristen can teach you a thing or two about the business of marketing plans and maintaining control over client engagements.

When you're good at something your clients will ask you to do things that are outside your wheelhouse. Completely natural.

So how do we say "no" to clients that want to give you more business? We don't, we use the opportunity to our advantage.

Simply find and introduce people that focus in that particular area!

- Stay in your lane
- Build trust as an advisor
- Build new strategic partnerships

Watch Kristen Ortwerth's full interview. We talk about barriers, the anatomy of marketing plans for software companies, vendor evaluation and simple solutions to big problems.

https://bit.ly/KristenOrtwerth

CO-CREATION

Like a pro coach or a pirate captain, losing control means we walk the plank.

As a strategist, indispensable partner and decision maker we must maintain control during the four stages of problem solving, each with its own challenges and opportunities.

Stage 1: Information Gathering
Stage 2: Strategy / Planning
Stage 3: Implementation
Stage 4: Asses & Refine

During each stage our clients challenge us. They do this unconsciously. They are wild, untrained beasts. We don't blame them, we just know how to handle them. There are no bad dogs, just bad owners.

A challenge occurs AFTER a decision is made without us. It's the tip of the iceberg.

When a client says we need to get the pay-per-click campaign started before the strategy is done, that means a decision was made without you.

The process of co-creation is how we stop this from happening. It's a proactive solution.

It works like this: ego prevents our clients from taking our advice. Our ideas will always be met with challenges. The solution is to make our clients think our ideas are really their ideas.

This happens through a controlled process of co-creation:

1. We know the answer ahead of time, but we don't reveal it
2. We ask the client questions, leading them to said answer
3. Enjoy

Best Case: client thinks our idea is theirs and they don't challenge us

Worst Case: they have a better idea and we secure our position as a value add in the decision making process

Either way, win or lose, we maintain control.

The best consultants complete their recommendations before the co-creation process.

Before:

- Workshops
- Brain Storms
- Performance Analysis
- "Sprint meetings" for those of you on the EOS bandwagon

My advice is to prepare your recommendations as though your client has zero say in the matter. Then create a copy of your completed deliverable, delete your recommendations and leave only the structure: blank spaces for their ideas.

This "backup" plan will function as a confidence boost and a conversation guide. Ask questions until you get the answer you want or a better one.

TRUTH: No Control = No Margin

When do you get the most pushback from clients?

HINT: Run "Co-Creation workshops" on these topics to eliminate pushbacks.

Tamsen Webster

Former TEDx Executive Producer turned messaging consultant & creator of The Red Thread™ methodology for idea messaging.

"A lot of times our ideas and our messages are not in sync. We have a great idea, and we know it's great, but we have a really hard time getting other people to agree that it's great."

My take:

Selling ideas is hard work because they are much harder to explain than tangible work products.

I think most marketers would agree that planning, strategy & ideas should be sold, but they struggle to explain why clients need it, what they get, and the work process.

Without messaging and process ideas fall flat. We panic and revert back to what we are comfortable selling and what the client is asking for: the "doing".

Tamsen is brilliant. I highly recommend listening to her explain The Red Thread™.

https://bit.ly/TamsenWebster

BREAKING THE HABIT

Commit, sell, deliver.

Without a personal commitment to break through the plateau we won't risk our next deal. We're too hungry to resist an easy meal.

"The next thing I sell will be a plan."

Say it!
smack
SAY IT!!

With a personal commitment we MIGHT hold ourselves accountable to sell a new idea. The idea needs enough thought behind it to set and meet the expectations of our first "pilot" client. We need to answer the basic client questions like "why do I need it", "what do I get" and "how do we work together". This amounts to a couple page proposal for strategic services.

When that first client cuts us a check they tap into our very best: our deeply rooted motivation to impress our clients and give them more than their money's worth.

This process of "sell then build" tricks our mind to focus on creating something new, hitching a ride on what we do naturally: make our clients happy.

For years I thought that agency owners and consultants would take the plunge, build and sell strategy because of the clear value to our organizations and their personal wellbeing.

Not true. Fear and hunger prevails 99% of the time.

Turns out the only thing that beats fear and hunger is values. We don't change because it benefits ourselves. We risk going hungry and we step into the void for our clients' benefit ONLY.

That is the mind trick. Sell it first. Sell the minimum viable product: because the obligation to deliver for a client is the only way to overcome your natural resistance to change.

BEWARE OF FEEDBACK

The more focused we get the more our ideal customers will see indispensable value. On the flipside non-ideal customers won't get it.

Feedback and observations from paying clients are gold. They should drive all product development past our initial idea and minimum viable product.

Feedback from anyone other than paying clients is dangerous: it dulls the blade.

Right now my editor is asking me to explain this concept further. I don't know how.

We need to be CUSTOMER focused!

NOT friendly advice focused,
NOT competitor posing as mentor focused,
NOT partner manager at big software company focused,

Just people that pay you money focused. What more do you want from me?

GIVE YOUR "THING" A NAME

There is a single answer to the question:

"What is the most valuable thing I know how to do?"

The answer lies at the center of your life experiences, not in research or a mentor's advice.

Ask yourself three simple questions:

Who have you helped?
How did you help them?
What made YOU so damn good at it?

The most powerful combination is where you should focus. Give it a name. Make it a thing.

Give yourself permission to sell the wrong thing. Remember the 90/10 rule. 90% of the value comes from the act of focusing, 10% comes from choosing the right thing.

The more specific the better.
What am I Selling Again?

RESULTS!

Your contribution to results is the "thing": an actionable plan that guides the implementation team.

An actionable plan requires:

- a clear objective
- education (for buy-in)
- resources
- directions

SELLING VS. BUYING

We have to understand that implementation services are BOUGHT. As agencies we hope to "win" these deals by beating our immediate competition and the infamous "no decision".

To sell strategy, we must first help the client identify what is most important, which is never what they ask for in the first place.

If you help them discover what is most important you gain permission to present a unique solution: strategy, planning, ideas.

We have trouble selling strategy initially because we're out of practice.

With practice strategy can be easier and much faster to sell because you have a solution that is most important and cannot be replaced by others.

The important thing to remember is not to get discouraged. Most of your ideal clients aren't looking to buy strategy so we have to be proactive. This is a big shift for most professional service organizations that have traditionally reacted to requests for proposals.

Reactional vs Intentional.

DISQUALIFICATION

Speaking with people who don't value planning and strategy is dangerous. Not only is it a waste of time but you risk misinterpreting the needs of your ideal customers and you risk taking on bad clients.

The truth is: taking on a bad client is far worse than losing a deal because of the psychological impact and time investment. You can always win another deal but you can't get your time back.

Therefore we need to be experts at identifying bad fit clients as early as possible in the sales process. In this case "bad fit" has nothing to do with our chosen focus or expertise. We are looking for a mindset mismatch.

A truly bad fit client does not value our greatest contribution. There is a mismatch between our identity and their perceived value.

Disqualification is easy if we declare our greatest contribution up front. It sounds like this:

"Hi, I'm Max, I create marketing plans".

It's an oversimplification but it gets the job done. Clear from the beginning.

Yeah, yeah, I know you want to start with VALUE:

"Hi, I'm Max, I help companies grow by ensuring their marketing investments turn into sales".

Sounds good right? Wrong! The enemy of value is replaceability. That value prop jargon crap just sounds like "marketer" to the client.

"Oh, you do marketing. I've hired people like you before. They sucked".

Conversation goes nowhere. I call this the "dog-shit-bucket".

Try again. Be clear. State your identity. Be different. Peak their interest.

"Wait, you only do plans? I don't get it, I need someone to do the work".

NOW you have an opportunity to position the DIFFERENTIATED value.

"Yeah most people hire marketers or agencies without a plan. They spend a bunch of money and get crappy results. It's a big problem. A little planning can go a long way in turning bad investments into good ones".

Never end on a statement. Ask that leading question:

"What's been your experience"? Let the games begin.

TAMSEN WEBSTER'S "RATIONALIZATION TRAP"

The rationalization trap is a concept I learned from Tamsen Webster which she discusses at length in the Beers with Max interview a few pages back.

Humans are not rational decision makers, they are RATIONALIZING decision makers. When faced with a decision they will look for reasons NOT to do it. Any reason NOT to do it will overpower all reasons for doing it.

In other words any one piece of your idea can kill the deal.

It's a pickle. In order to feel confident in selling our idea we need to know everything about it... everything the client gets, how it's used, each itty bitty step in the process. We take comfort in detail and we jump at the opportunity to share that detail with our prospective clients.

BUT, under the rationalization trap, more detail offers more reasons to say no. They pick out one thing they already have or they don't believe they need and it kills the entire deal.

So as you build your first proposal, keep the extreme detail to yourself. Clients need to see a simplified version to reduce the odds of falling into the rationalization trap.

| All the stuff you know they need | — | Reason NOT to buy |

CONVERSATIONS, NOT CONTENT.

With focus we've got something that a certain type of someone will pay a LOT of money for. Everyone else could care less. This means the days of waiting around for Prince Charming to fill out a form on your website are over. We need to take responsibility for our sales pipeline.

Intentional outreach is steak.

Inbound leads are pepper.

Pepper makes steak taste better but we sure as hell can't survive on pepper alone!

I just finished reviewing my sales pipeline for all of 2019:

10,000 prospective organizations researched (according to category and keyword),
1000 cold outreach messages on Linkedin **(10%),**
200 people agreed to have a conversation with me **(20%),**
150 video call conversations actually took place averaging 20 minutes each **(75%),**
75 of those conversations turned into opportunities, defined by having an interest in how I could help them **(50%),**
16 new clients **(21%).**

The numbers are VERY good for a few reasons:

1. All 10,000 people were picked by human beings (in India) looking for very specific criteria across websites and social profiles: meaning all 1000 were a perfect fit, 90% were NOT a fit.
2. All 1000 outreach messages were hand written by humans (in the US), based on templates, but human enough to pass the test.
3. Every outreach message was an invitation to contribute to my podcast (beers with max), my book (5 years in the making) or my research... still working on that one.

4. Not every conversation turned into content but every single piece of content I created, by definition, involved a conversation with an ideal buyer.

The truth is: we've all got content marketing backwards:

Content doesn't get you conversations.
Conversations get you content.

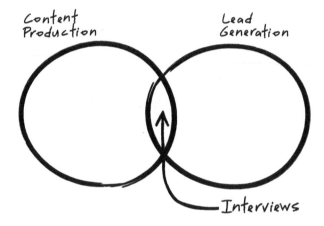

BEER

This was the title of the 1000 unsolicited "cold" Linkedin messages that drove 100% of my income in 2019:

"Would you like to have a beer?"

Explain that.

Our inboxes are saturated with robots. "Automation" allows us to reach thousands with the stroke of a key.

On one hand: people get turned off.
On the other: people can tell when a human is reaching out.

The truth is: robots don't drink beer, so my message gets through because I'm human.

50% of my conversations turned into opportunities.

Again, I credit beer. Not because people like me more when they're drunk, although that might be true, but because of what beer represents.

No stress,
No preparation,
No fear.

When I drink beer with someone and talk about business there's no pressure: just two people sharing stories trying to figure out if we can stomach a conversation.

Turns out 50% of people who enjoy YOU as a person will consider working with you.

Matt Heinz
President, Heinz Marketing Inc, Keynote speaker,
Author, Host of Sales Pipeline Radio

"You can't just sit and wait for your dream client to show up on Google. You lose all control of your pipeline, business, and margin."

My take:

I've looked up to Matt for a long time from a personal brand standpoint. He generates more inbound leads than most of us ever will.

Is every inbound lead an ideal customer? No.

When you shout from your porch with a megaphone you have very little control over who knocks on your door.

Who cares? More leads are better right? Wrong.

Matt is the brilliant strategist as well as the sales guy. When Matt spends an hour on the phone with a bad fit prospect, he doesn't get that time back.

Inbound leads are a bonus.

Make a list of ideal customers, be proactive, know the numbers.

Watch Matt Heinz's full interview. He talks about the right way to approach sales and marketing.

https://bit.ly/MattHeinz30

PART IV

———

THE ROAD TO RESIDUAL INCOME

Each progressive model offers less control over the process requiring better documentation and supporting content.

The reward is a higher revenue ceiling and lower cost structure so you can take your kid to Disney World and the business doesn't eat while you sleep.

DING

Let's rewind for a second. Back in 2013, before I left my agency...

Those HubSpot clients didn't cancel once they had a plan. Some of them actually upped their subscriptions to access more features.

So, Hubspot asked us to teach other value added resellers (agencies) how to stop clients from cancelling their software subscriptions.

The "churn program" they called it.

We stumbled into a licensing model.

The agencies paid us to learn how to use our workshop and strategy templates.

Then they paid us 20% every time they did it for a customer.

On average the agencies we licenced the process to would sell it for $5,000 or $10,000.

So here's me: 25 years old, working my ass off at an agency of ten people with piss poor profit margins and constant client fires.

All of a sudden I'm waking up in the middle of the night because one of my Australian licensees keeps selling the Content Marketer's Blueprint™!

I set my phone to *ding* whenever I get an email from PayPal.

ding goes $1,000

ding goes $2,000...

then I wake up and sit in traffic for an hour to babysit angry clients and flight risk millennials?

NO FRIENDS AT CAMP RESIDUAL

The first time I spoke about the "agency death spiral" there were twenty agencies in the audience, all in the traditional "time and materials" model.

Just a week prior I attended a presentation with the very same group. The topic was profit margins so I knew that most of them were taking away less than five percent of revenue. The bigger they got, the worse the margins. I came to find that this group was a fair representation of the hundreds I would interview and work with in the years to come.

I've done a lot of public speaking, but never in my life had I gotten such unanimous and emotional backlash. Granted I try to be as opinionated as possible during these talks, but still.

"YOU ARE WRONG!"

Grown business owners acting like children being told Santa isn't real.

I learned that most people are emotionally attached to this broken model regardless of how painful it is.

As you begin your journey down the Digital, Scalable, Residual road you will share your excitement with others and you will be surprised to learn the same thing I did:

90% of people don't get it.

In this final section I want to show you the three major stages of your new business model and the roadblocks along the way. No need to rush, one stage naturally leads to another and jumping ahead too quickly will likely put you in your place.

That said, the hardest thing about following the road is the lack of support from your "old model peers".

STRATEGIC COACH™

Strategic Coach is a workshop style coaching organization for entrepreneurs created by Dan Sullivan. I joined back in 2015, five years ago as I write this.

It has provided a structured support network of entrepreneurs that create new revenue streams their competitors never knew existed.

We need to surround ourselves with people who are TRYING to break out of their traditional business models because if the only people you talk to are telling you:

"YOU'RE WRONG",

you'll start to believe them.

STOP #1: PRODUCTIZED CONSULTING SERVICE

Sell strategy, consulting, planning: "Think" not "do".

This is where price premiums survive in even the most saturated of markets.

Treat the service like a product. Every engagement has consistent inputs, time & resources, and consistent outputs: deliverables & results.

We customize the product for every client: just like our iPhone. But, every client is put through the same process.

Under this model WE do the thinking for our clients.

It is the highest cost, lowest margin model because of our involvement, but it offers the greatest opportunity for innovation and product development to support more scalable models.

Every client engagement under this model will improve the value we create for clients and the efficiency with which we can deliver it. Because of this we have to maintain at least one direct client relationship under the productized consulting service model, else we lose our grip on reality.

Supply and demand: as we reduce the number of clients we work with directly we can charge more.

If people want to work with the "creator" directly it will cost them a premium.

STOP #2: FACILITATED PROCESS

"Teach" them to "think".

The major difference between a consulting service and a facilitated process is who does the thinking.

Our clients can think for themselves, they just need to be guided through the thought process.

Unlike a productized consulting service which must be tailored to individual client challenges, a facilitated process can be delivered to multiple (similar) organizations at once because all the customization is done by the recipient of the service, not the facilitator.

Strategic Coach^{TM} is a facilitator process. I fly to Toronto. I sit in a room with 30 other entrepreneurs with similar challenges and objectives. A certified facilitator leads the group through a structured thinking process. I think for myself.

I pay about $9,000CA (Canadian Dollars) a year for this.

This model is much happier at scale than a productized consulting service.

    1. One facilitator services many clients.
    2. Multiple facilitators allow the product to reach more people.

Dan Sullivan, the creator, runs one group. It costs about $25,000CA dollars a year.

Supply and demand.

STOP #3: LICENSED PROCESS

"Teach" another company to "teach" their customers how to "think".

The difference between a facilitated process and a licenced process is who gets the overhead.

Strategic Coach has a sales team, they take on the cost of sale.
Strategic Coach has facilitators, they take on the cost of delivery.

A licenced process puts the burden of overhead onto the licensee.
A "licensee" is the person paying for the ability to sell someone else's product to their customers.

"EOS" The Entrepreneurial Operating System™ created by Gino Wickman, author of *Traction* and *Rocket Fuel* is a licenced process.

NOTE: These figures represent educated estimates.
Professional EOS implementers pay $25,000 to be certified by EOS Worldwide over a two day workshop.

They pay $1,000 per month to maintain their certification, granting them access to additional training and support material delivered through an online learning management system.

The implementers maintain their own independent businesses, they do the selling, they charge what they want and they stop when they want.

EOS Worldwide is a marketing powerhouse because they focus on innovation and marketing, not sales and consulting. They attract end clients with books like *Traction* and *Rocket Fuel.*

As a BONUS, and this is my very favorite part:

When the end clients ask for help implementing the EOS methodology, EOS Worldwide flips the opportunity to a certified implementer for an undisclosed "finders fee", which is not uncommon to exceed 50% of revenue in comparable sales methodologies.

Last time I checked EOS has over 250 professional implementers. You do the math.

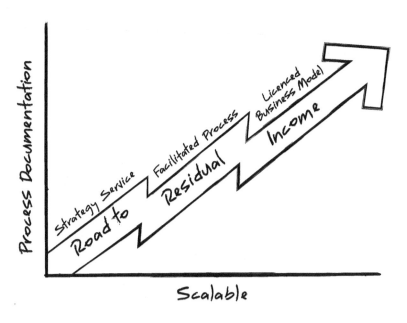

NO SUCH THING AS HANDS OFF

For some reason everyone and their mothers are creating relatively low-cost "hands-off" video courses. When you see a video course under $1,000 it means there is little to no hands-on support in the business model.

Theory is: someone will watch the videos and do the work. Maybe ask some questions to a facebook group that will be answered by other people taking the course.

If everyone on earth was an A-student this would work out well. But we know that isn't true.

Most B-students simply lack the motivation to be an A-student. We have the smarts but we don't do the work.

In the business world, people don't take action on "hands-off" online classes because:

1. They have a lot of other things to do
2. It didn't cost that much, so they don't feel strongly obligated to finish
3. Nobody is holding them accountable, which is especially true for people in "boss" positions, which happens to be the target for most of these business courses.

The truth is there's no such thing as hands-off. Everyone needs someone to hold them accountable. That someone's job is to understand and reinforce the client's personal motivation. The accountability role is not expensive, relative to hiring a one-to-one consultant, but it's something.

Generally, courses above $1,000 have strong accountability roles built in.

BEWARE: THE ONLINE COURSE MODEL

It works for some no doubt, but not US!

Like me, you feed your kids by selling high price services at low volume.

Selling low price services at high volume is VERY different.

Agency owners that develop an online course will blow the entirety of their innovation efforts on creating this new product. That's a fact.

Most will not sell enough units to justify further investment in the product, so they revert back to spending a majority of their time on the clients who still pay them under the old model and the product just sits there.

I mean at least it doesn't cost them anything for a video course to just sit there and do nothing, but the real problem is that this experience will prevent them from ever leaving the broken professional services model.

"We tried that, it didn't work" they say.

If this is you and you're cringing right now because we haven't met and I'm looking directly into your soul, then try this:

Instead of SELLING your course as a theoretical lead-in product to your high-ticket consulting service, try it the other way around.

Sell your high-ticket consulting. Do the thing you KNOW you can do. Then once you deliver your strategy to a happy client, tell them about your certification program for the employees and team members who can improve, maintain and implement the strategy for the organization.

Sales consultancies have been doing this for decades. They sell the strategy, they call it a "sales playbook", then sell licences to online training for all the individual reps to the tune of hundreds, potentially thousands of seats at a time.

I like starting with big ticket strategy & consulting to ensure everyone I work with has money and is willing to spend it to solve their problem.

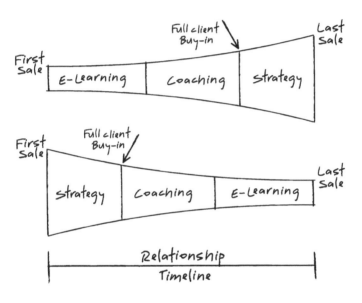

Tony Hughes

Top sales influencer (Asia Pacific), keynote speaker & author of The Joshua Principle: Leadership Secrets of Selling.

"The Dream is to get away from time for money and productize IP."

My take:

Success in the wrong business model will kill you, as it nearly killed Tony.

Tony has an incredibly powerful personal brand. He's got no problem finding clients. His is an amplified case of demand outweighing energy. We rise to the occasion until it kills us.

"Good problems" we rationalize.

Well, guess what, your health is not something to be rationalized. And without a digital, scalable, and residual business model to grow into: we eventually break under the pressure.

My advice: plan on success, or success just might kill you.

Listen to Tony Hughes' full interview. We talk about pipeline, personal branding and the life changing event that forced him to break the time-for-money vortex.

https://bit.ly/TonyHughes

SUSTAINABLE VALUE

"The one thing that drags people away from long-term relevance is that they spend their best efforts on a single client instead of developing perspectives and processes for all their clients."
— DAVID C BAKER | *Business of Expertise*

Entrepreneurs contribute five categories of value to their organization, but only two of these categories will help you sustain value into the future.

Innovation & Marketing
Both are "one to many" contributions. They are value creators and profit generators. Innovation makes your product(s) better, faster and cheaper to deliver which benefits all current and future clients. Marketing launches that value out into the marketplace, educating and attracting the market to your solution. You might recognize these categories as working "ON" the business vs "IN" the business.

The truth is:
"Marketing and innovation produce results; all the rest are costs"
— PETER DRUCKER

Consulting and Sales
Both are "one to one" contributions. They deliver value and generate revenue one client at a time. We need to build systems around these contributions so others can take over. Don't let your work "IN" the business prevent you from working "ON" the business.

Administrative
One to zero. No value creation. No value delivery. These activities are a necessary cost of doing business. We need to delegate these activities.

TIME TRACKING

I can guarantee that the BIGGEST things holding you back from long-term relevance are written on the previous two pages.

You don't know the half of it!
Unless you track your time working "ON" and "IN" the business, it's impossible to know what categories are getting a majority of your time and energy.

Left unaware, we naturally spend most of our time on consulting and sales: selfless and hungry respectively. Administrative is next and the all- important innovation/marketing is last.

No excuses. All excuses are ridiculous. You need to understand where your time is going. It is the single most valuable, expensive, and finite resource you have. All you have to do is set up your categories and push a button when you start and stop a task.

Once a quarter look at where your time goes. Pick the biggest time suck in consulting, sales, or administration and delegate it.

I've got a video on how to set up Toggl, a free time tracking app. I'll also invite you to attend the workshops I hold for all my clients each quarter to help them identify what needs to go.

Just email me at max@maxtraylor.com and say "I want to be more productive."

DELEGATE DELEGATION TO A SIDEKICK

Every superhero needs a sidekick. A sidekick isn't an underpaid intern! They have superpowers of their own but they use their superpower to support their superhero.

The most important hire you will ever make is your sidekick. They have three responsibilities:

1. Your personal *productivity*
2. Product and service *profitability*
3. Managing *relationships* which impact productivity and profitability

We struggle to delegate things for two reasons.

First, we've gotten good at things we don't like doing.
Second, the person we delegate to is the wrong person.

A sidekick helps identify what SHOULD be delegated, creates the systems required, and finds the right person to do it.

If you suck at delegating, get help.

Mark S.A. Smith

Business Growth Strategist | Author | Host of Executive
Strategy & Leadership Skills Summit

"Executives never have to fight the same fire twice. If you're constantly fixing the same problem, you have a broken system."

My take:

The smartest people are their own worst enemy.

The things we do "because we can" come at a cost and that cost is always innovation.

Listen to Mark S.A. Smith's full interview. We talk about how entrepreneurs can grow by thinking like executives.

https://bit.ly/MarkSASmith30

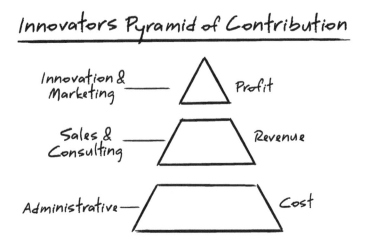

FASTER

The better your documentation, the faster you can jump to more Digital, Scalable, and Residual business models.

Jumping from one to the next without proper documentation will result in a "stall".

A buddy of mine, Robb, sold a facilitated process to sixty (60) clients at once during an industry event he was speaking at. He vanished for six months, not a word.

When he finally de-briefed me on what happened:

"We screwed up one thing in the process. Then we got calls from 60 clients who couldn't figure it out. We made a lot of money, but we barely survived".

It took six months to solve 60 problems because of one mistake in documentation.

At the end of the day we all have to learn these things for ourselves. Was it worth it for Robb? Yes.

Three types of documentation will dull the Digital, Scalable, and Residual growing pains:

1. Templates: input and output documents
2. Standard Operating Procedure (SOP): step by step directions
3. Feedback: from paying customers

RECORDED VIDEO CALLS

A very large percentage of human communication is body language. I don't know the exact figure, I'm not a scientist. A quick Google is telling me 55% is visual and 93% is "non-verbal" which includes visual.

Anyway, the single biggest source of paying client feedback is recorded video calls.

If a client bites their nails it means you're telling them something that makes them nervous.

If they look down and take notes it means you're telling them something they want to remember.

Recorded video calls tell you a lot more than interviews and surveys. It is the single biggest source of innovative ideas when it comes to making your process better, faster, and cheaper to deliver.

THE GAP

Why is it that everyone thinks we're brilliant yet we consider ourselves to be a total failure? The world sees us in front yet in our heads we're way behind.

It happens to visionaries. We succeed in business because we can imagine things others cannot. The downside of being a visionary is that our vision always exceeds our reality.

If you reach your vision, don't you cease to be a visionary?

It's a paradox.

"The Gap" is something I learned from Dan Sullivan's Strategic Coach™ program, but it's something I've felt my entire life. This gap is the space between where you are and your unattainable vision.

When we measure ourselves in The Gap we're always behind, always failures, always chasing something bigger.

The key is to avoid the gap: it's not a fun place to be.

A simple mindset shift will make your visionary adventures a lot more fun: measure your progress.

Looking backwards you're always a hero. This is the way the world perceives visionaries.

Join them.

IMPOSTER SYNDROME

The more we learn the less we know.

At least that's what our brain tells us.

Example:
Marketing has ten topical areas to master.

You have mastered three topics and you have no idea the other seven exist.

You're confident in your marketing knowledge. From your perspective you know everything.

Then one day you discover areas of marketing you've never explored.

At this moment everyone, including you, would agree that you are smarter than the moment prior. You have acquired new knowledge and yet your confidence is shattered.

Imposter Syndrome benefits nobody!

What we fail to realize in moments of paralyzing imposter syndrome is that our clients know less than we do. There are probably people out there who have mastered all topics, but they aren't here right now!

So what choice do you have?
Let the client lead the way? No
Wait for the self proclaimed marketer of the world to show up? Mr. Ten? No

You are your clients' best shot. So be a leader, be confident.

EMOTIONAL BREAKDOWNS

You'll be tired, hungry, and feeling like you know nothing and your dream reality is slipping away. You should have listened to your "old model friends". Maybe you are a bit crazy.

A breakdown happens when you can't bring yourself to do the things you love to do.

So take a break.

It will happen more and more until one day you realize it's just a part of stepping into the void and doing something new.

The truth is: you ARE crazy, just like the rest of us.

Cheers!

Raise your glass and make a toast to our fallen peers...
those who stuck with a dying model to the very end...
we salute you.

LAST CALL

Don't forget to:

- Put your personal life first
- Charge for strategy
- Be intentional with your pipeline
- Create repeatable systems
- Celebrate progress
- RELAX: have a drink!

NEED A RIDE?

Susan Tatum
susan@theconversioncompany.com
She'll fill your pipeline with conversations.

Jonathan Rivera
jonathan@thepodcastfactory.com
He'll help you create a podcast and turn interviews into a book.

Katrina Busselle
katrina@katrinabusselle.com
She'll find you a #2 so you can do more of what you do best.

Tamsen Webster
tamsen@tamsenwebster.com
She'll help you create a minimum viable message for your idea.